CONTENTS

WITHDRAWN FROM STOCK

D0236139

INTRODUCTION

Hanging baskets turn gardeners into magicians as they move gardening from the ground to mid-air. They draw the eye and provide the finishing touch to a summer garden, as well as adding seasonal colour and interest to the dullest of winter walls and the most difficult of corners.

Each hanging basket is a miniature garden with its own soil conditions, micro-climate and plants. Like all containers, hanging baskets give the gardener the opportunity to ignore the limitations of problem soil types and create the perfect conditions for a long-lasting display of flowers and foliage. Hanging baskets can be assembled in an instant with mature plants or, more economically, grown on from smaller plants early in the season. Whichever way you choose, there is the satisfaction of seeing a concentration of colour which can seldom be achieved with the same intensity elsewhere in the garden.

You do not need to be an expert to create successful hanging baskets and you certainly do not need a large garden or lots of equipment – a bracket, a basket, some moss and compost, a few plants and you are ready to create your own hanging garden.

BASIC TECHNIQUES

Seed Sowing

Some plants are very easy to sow from seed – nasturtiums rarely disappoint, even if you are a complete beginner.

1 Fill the pot with seed compost. Gently firm and level the surface by pressing down on the compost using a pot of the same size.

2 When sowing large seeds, such as sunflowers or nasturtiums, use a dibber, cane or pencil to make holes for each seed. Plant the seeds and then firmly tap the side of the pot with the flat of your hand to fill the holes with compost. Water from above, using a fine rose on a watering can, or by standing the pot in a saucer of water until the surface of the compost is moist. Cover the pot with a black plastic bag as most seeds germinate best in a warm dark place. Check daily and bring into the light when the seedlings are showing.

3 When sowing small seeds they should be thinly scattered on the surface of the compost and then covered with just enough sieved compost to conceal them. Firm the surface, using another pot, and then treat in the same way as large seeds.

Potting-on

Sooner or later, plants need repotting. Young seedlings, shown here, do not thrive in over-large pots. Divide the plants, if necessary, and plant them in pots the same size as the one they were previously grown in.

1 Seedlings will probably be ready to move into larger pots when the roots start to emerge through the holes in the base of the pot. To check, gently remove the rootball from the pot and, if there are plenty of roots showing, you will know the plants are ready for a move.

2 If there is more than one seedling in the pot, gently break each seedling away with a good rootball. (Some plants hate to have their roots disturbed. The information on the seed packet will tell you this. These seeds are best sown individually in peat pots.)

3 Lower the rootball of the plant into the pot and gently pour compost around it, lightly pressing the compost around the roots and stem. It does not matter if the stem of the seedling is buried deeper than it was previously as long as the leaves are well clear of the soil. Water, using a can with a fine rose.

Watering

Too much water is as bad as too little – get the balance right and your plants will thrive.

1. Hanging baskets need a good soaking with a watering can or hose before they are hung in position.

2. Summer hanging baskets need daily watering even in overcast weather and on a hot day should be watered morning and evening. Once they have been allowed to dry out it can be difficult for the compost to re-absorb water. In these circumstances it is a good idea to immerse baskets in a large bucket or bowl of water.

3. Winter and spring hanging baskets should be watered only when the soil is dry. Container composts include a water- retaining gel and if the compost remains wet in cold weather it can cause the roots to rot.

Preparing the Basket

The key to successful hanging baskets is in the preparation. Time taken in preparing the basket for planting will be rewarded with a long-lasting colourful display. Slow-release plant food granules incorporated into the compost when planting will ensure that the plants receive adequate nutrients throughout the growing season. It is essential to water hanging baskets every day, even in overcast weather, as they dry out very quickly. There are various ways to line a hanging basket, but the most attractive and successful is to use moss. All of the baskets in this book are lined with sphagnum moss – available from most garden centres and good florists.

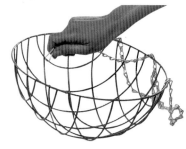

When buying a hanging basket, make sure that the chains are detachable. Unhooking one of the chains enables them to be placed to one side of the basket, allowing you to work freely.

Alternative Linings

If you cannot find sphagnum moss, or if you want to use something else to line your baskets, there are other options.

1 Although not as good to look at as moss, coir fibre lining is soon hidden as the plants grow. The slits allow for planting in the side of the basket.

2 Cardboard liners are clean and easy to use. They are made in various sizes to fit most hanging baskets.

3 Press out the marked circles on the cardboard liner if you wish to plant into the side of it.

Underplanting a Hanging Basket

Underplanting helps to achieve a really lush-looking basket and soon conceals the shape of the container under flowers and foliage.

1 Line the lower half of the basket with a generous layer of moss.

2 Gently guide the foliage through the sides of the basket and rest the rootball on the moss.

3 Add more moss to the basket, tucking it carefully around the plants to ensure that they are firmly in place. Add a further row of plants near the top edge of the basket, if required, and continue to line the basket with moss, finishing off with a collar of moss overlapping the rim of the basket. Fill with compost.

Planting a Wall Basket

The principle of planting a wall basket is the same as an ordinary one, but for maximum effect it is always a good idea to underplant as well to give a good display of colour against the wall.

Planting a Hanging Basket

1 Tease out the moss and fill the bowl of the basket with a generous layer. It is important to make sure there are no holes or compost and water will escape.

2 Build a thick collar of moss overlapping the rim of the basket. This will ensure that water soaks into the basket rather than running off the surface.

1 Line the back and lower half of the front of the basket with moss.

2 Plant some of your chosen plants into the side of the basket by resting the rootballs on the moss and feeding the foliage through. Add another layer of soil and moss and plant more plants.

3 Complete lining the basket with moss and fill with compost mixture and any slow-release feed you may wish to use. Plant the rest of your plants, starting at the centre and working out to the sides.

3 Fill the basket with compost.

Common Pests

Aphids
One of the most common plant pests, these sap-sucking insects feed on the tender growing tips of plants. Most insecticides are effective against aphids such as greenfly or blackfly (*shown above*). Choose one that will not harm ladybirds.

Mealy bugs
These look like spots of white mould. They are hard to shift and regular treatment with a systemic insecticide is the best solution.

Caterpillars
The occasional caterpillar can simply be picked off the plant and disposed of as you see fit, but a major infestation can strip a plant before your eyes. Contact insecticides are usually very effective in these cases.

Red spider mite
This is an insect that thrives indoors in dry conditions. Constant humidity will reduce the chance of an infestation. The spider mite is barely visible to the human eye, but infestation is indicated by the presence of fine webs and mottling of the plant's leaves. To treat an infestation, pick off the worst affected leaves and spray the plants with an insecticide.

Vine weevils
These white grubs are a real problem. The first sign of an infestation is the sudden collapse of the plant, which has died as a result of the weevil eating its roots. Systemic insecticides or natural predators can be used as a preventative, but once a plant has been attacked it is usually too late to save it. Never re-use the soil from an affected plant. The picture above shows an adult weevil.

Snails
Snails are not generally a problem in hanging baskets unless there is overhanging foliage by which they can travel. They are more of a problem in wall baskets, where they can tuck themselves behind the basket during daylight and venture out to feast at night. Slug pellets should deal with them or, alternatively, you can venture out yourself with a torch and catch them.

Whitefly
As their name indicates, these are tiny white flies which flutter up in clouds when disturbed from their feeding places on the undersides of leaves. Whitefly are particularly troublesome in conservatories, where a dry atmosphere will encourage them to breed. Keep the air as moist as possible. Contact insecticides will need more than one application to deal with an infestation, but a systemic insecticide will protect the plant for weeks.

Insecticides

There are two main types of insecticide available
to combat common pests.

Contact insecticides

These must be sprayed directly on
to the insects to be effective. Most
organic insecticides work this
way, but they generally kill all
insects, even beneficial ones, such
as hoverflies and ladybirds. Try to
remove these before spraying the
infected plant.

Systemic insecticides

These work by being absorbed by the plant's root
or leaf system and killing insects that come into
contact with the plant. This will work for difficult
pests, such as the grubs of vine weevils which are
hidden in the soil, and scale insects which protect
themselves from above with a scaly cover.

Biological control

Commercial growers now
use biological control in
their glasshouses; this means
natural predators are
introduced to eat the pest
population. Although not all
are suitable for the amateur
gardener, they can be used
in conservatories for dealing
with pests such as whitefly.

Composts

Composts come in various formulations suitable for different plant requirements. A standard potting compost is usually peat-based and is suitable for all purposes. Different composts can be mixed together for specific plant needs.

Loam-based compost (1)
This uses sterilized loam as the main ingredient, with fertilizers to supplement the nutrients in the loam. Although much heavier than peat-based compost, it can be lightened by mixing with peat-free compost.

Ericaceous compost (2)
A peat-based compost with no added lime, this is essential for rhododendrons, camellias and heathers in containers.

Peat-free compost (3)
Manufacturers are beginning to offer composts using materials from renewable resources such as coir fibre.

Standard compost (4)
Most composts available at garden centres are peat-based with added fertilizers.

Container compost (5)
This is a peat-based compost with moisture-retaining granules and added fertilizer, specially formulated for hanging baskets and containers.

Feeding your Plants

It is not generally known that most potting composts only contain sufficient food for six weeks of plant growth. After that, the plants will slowly starve unless other food is introduced. There are several products available, all of which are easy to use.

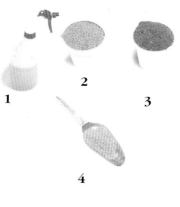

Slow-release plant food granules (above left, nos 2, 3 and 4)
These will keep your plants in prime condition and are very easy to use. One application lasts six months, whereas most other plant foods need to be applied fortnightly.

Liquid feeds (top left, no 1)
These are available in many formulations. Generally, the organic liquid manures and seaweed feeds are brown in colour and should be mixed to look like very weak tea. The chemical feeds are frequently coloured to prevent them being mistaken for soft drinks. The best way to avoid accidents with garden chemicals is to mix up only as much as you need on each occasion and never store them in soft-drinks bottles. Liquid feeds should be applied fortnightly in the growing season. Do not be tempted to mix a feed stronger than is recommended – it can burn the roots of the plant and it certainly will not make it grow any faster.

Water-retaining Gel

One of the main problems with hanging baskets is the amount of watering required to keep the plants thriving. Adding water-retaining gels to the compost will certainly help to reduce this task. Sachets of gel are available from garden centres.

3 Add to your compost at the recommended rate.

4 Mix the gel in thoroughly before using it for planting.

1 Pour the recommended amount of water into a bowl.

2 Scatter the gel over the surface, stirring occasionally until it has absorbed the water.

Tools

Very few tools are needed for working with hanging baskets. A couple of medium-size trowels, a small rake and a watering can are all you should need.

Hanging your Basket

When a hanging basket is fully planted and laden with wet compost, it is surprisingly heavy. For this reason it is important to make sure that your basket is supported by a strong metal bracket, which must be screwed into a brick or stone wall; a wooden wall or fence may not be strong enough to take the heavy weight.

Types of Hanging Basket

Before you choose the plants and how to arrange them, you need to decide what sort of hanging basket you are going to display them in. Garden centres stock a huge variety, which are all easy to work with and hang.

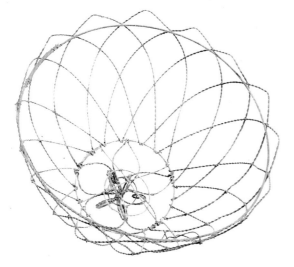

Baskets are generally made from plastic-coated wire, but are also available in wrought iron and galvanized wire.

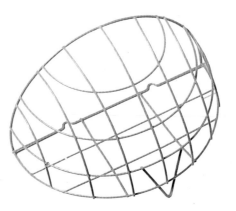

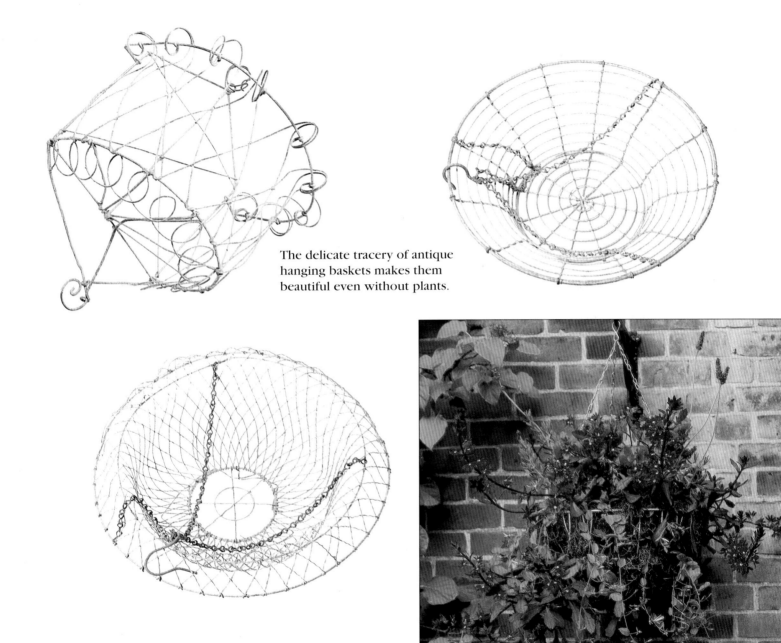

The delicate tracery of antique hanging baskets makes them beautiful even without plants.

It is now possible to buy copies of these antique wirework baskets although, when fully planted, most of your basket will be covered (*see right*).

GREEN BASKETS

An Evergreen Wall Basket

Pansies will flower throughout the winter. Even if they are flattened by rain, frost or snow, at the first sign of improvement in the weather their heads will pop up again to bring brightness to the dullest day. They have been planted with ivies to provide colour from early autumn through to late spring.

MATERIALS
30 cm (12 in) wall basket
Sphagnum moss
Compost

PLANTS
2 golden variegated ivies
2 copper pansies (*Viola*)
Yellow pansy (*Viola*)

pansy

ivy

GARDENER'S TIP

Winter baskets do not need regular feeding and should only be watered in very dry conditions. To prolong the flowering life of the pansies, dead-head regularly and pinch out any straggly stems to encourage new shoots from the base.

Plant in autumn

1 Line the basket with moss.

2 Three-quarters fill the basket with compost and position the ivies with their rootballs resting on the compost. Guide the stems through the sides of the basket so that they trail downwards. Pack more moss around the ivies and top up the basket with compost.

3 Plant the two copper pansies at either end of the basket.

4 Plant the yellow pansy in the centre of the basket. Water well and hang in shade or semi-shade.

Classic Winter Colours

Convolvulus cneorum is an attractive small shrub with eye-catching silver-grey leaves which last through winter and it has white flowers in spring and summer. Planted with ice-blue pansies, it makes a softly subtle display from autumn to spring.

MATERIALS
30 cm (12 in) hanging basket
Sphagnum moss
Compost

PLANTS
8 silver/blue pansies (*Viola*) 'Silver Wings', or similar
Convolvulus cneorum

Convolvulus

pansies

GARDENER'S TIP

At the end of winter cut back any dead wood or straggly branches on the *Convolvulus cneorum* and give a liquid feed to encourage new growth. Small shrubs such as this may be used in hanging baskets for one season, but will then need planting into a larger container or the border.

Plant in autumn

1 Half line the basket with moss and fill with compost to the top of the moss.

2 Plant four of the pansies into the side of the basket by placing their root balls on the compost and gently guiding the leaves through the side of the basket.

3 Line the rest of the basket with moss and top up with compost. Plant the *Convolvulus* in the centre of the basket.

4 Plant the remaining four pansies around the *Convolvulus*. Water well and hang in sun or partial shade.

Full of Ferns

A damp shady corner is the perfect position for a basket of ferns. Provided they are regularly fed and watered, and the ferns are cut back in late autumn, this basket will give pleasure for many years. We have chosen hardy ferns, but the idea can be adapted for a conservatory or bathroom using less hardy plants such as the maidenhair fern.

MATERIALS
36 cm (14 in) hanging basket
Sphagnum moss
Compost
Slow-release plant food granules

PLANTS
4 different ferns (we used
    *Dryopteris, Athyrium,
    Matteuccia struthiopteris*
    and *Asplenium crispum*)

Asplenium

Athyrium

Matteuccia

Dryopteris

1 Line the basket with moss.

2 Fill the basket with compost. Mix a teaspoon of slow-release plant food granules into the top of the compost.

GARDENER'S TIP
Strange as it may seem, finely chopped banana skins are a favourite food of ferns. Simply sprinkle around the base of the stems and watch the ferns flourish.

Plant in spring

3 Before removing the ferns from their pots, arrange them in the basket to ensure that you achieve a balanced effect.

4 Plant the ferns.

Beans in a Basket

Many of us, especially city dwellers, love the idea of growing a few vegetables, but limited space, insufficient sun and the predations of slugs and snails can make it a frustrating experience. A hanging basket devoted to dwarf beans and parsley can be surprisingly productive and will outwit all but the most acrobatic of snails.

MATERIALS
36 cm (14 in) hanging basket
Sphagnum moss
Compost
Slow-release plant food granules

PLANTS
7 parsley plants
3 dwarf bean plants

parsley

dwarf bean

1 Line the lower half of the basket with moss and fill with compost.

2 Plant the parsley into the sides of the basket, resting the rootballs on the compost and feeding the leaves through the sides.

GARDENER'S TIP

Fruit and vegetable hanging baskets need quite a lot of attention to crop well. They should be kept moist at all times and need a liquid feed once a week. If you are going to be away, move the basket into the shade, where it will not dry out so quickly.

Plant in spring

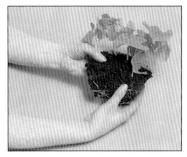

3 Gently separate the bean plants from one another.

4 Moss the upper half of the basket and add further compost. Mix a teaspoon of slow-release plant food granules into the top of the compost. Plant the beans in the compost. Water thoroughly and hang in partial sun.

A Hanging Garden of Herbs

A basket of herbs is both decorative and useful, especially when hung near the kitchen door or window. Herbs benefit from regular picking to encourage the plants to produce lots of tender new shoots throughout the summer. Some herbs can be very vigorous so be sure to choose compact varieties for your hanging basket.

MATERIALS
30 cm (12 in) hanging basket
Sphagnum moss
Compost
Slow-release plant food granules

PLANTS
5 parsley
French tarragon
Sage
Rosemary (prostrate form)
2 basil

parsley

basil

rosemary

French tarragon

sage

1 Line the lower half of the basket with moss.

4 Plant the sage.

2 Plant the parsley into the sides of the basket, resting the rootballs on the moss and feeding the leaves through the sides.

3 Line the rest of the basket with moss, ensuring it is tucked around the parsley plants, and fill the basket with compost. Mix a teaspoon of slow-release plant food granules into the top of the compost. Position the tarragon and plant.

5 Plant the prostrate form of rosemary, angling it slightly to encourage it to grow over the side of the basket.

GARDENER'S TIP

Fortunately, the strongly aromatic nature of most herbs does dissuade pests, but if you should have any problems be sure to use a safe organic pesticide. Soapy washing-up water can be used against greenfly.

Plant in spring

6 Finally, plant the two basil plants and water well before hanging in partial sun. A regular liquid feed is recommended.

A White Theme for an Antique Basket

An antique basket is not essential for this scheme, but the bowl shape makes an interesting variation. A small variety of dahlia, known as dahlietta, has large white flowers that blend with trailing verbenas and a begonia. Silver-leaved *Argyranthemum* brings a subtle touch of colour to the basket.

MATERIALS
36 cm (14 in) hanging basket
Sphagnum moss
Compost
Slow-release plant food granules

PLANTS
White *Begonia semperflorens*
3 white dahlietta
3 white trailing verbena
3 *Argyranthemum* 'Flamingo'

Begonia

trailing verbena

dahlietta

Argyranthemum

1 Line the basket with moss and fill with compost. Mix a teaspoon of slow-release plant food granules into the top of the compost.

2 Plant the begonia in the centre and position and plant the dahliettas around the begonia.

GARDENER'S TIP
Regular dead-heading of the flowers will keep the basket in tip-top condition. The slow-release plant food granules will give the flowers a regular supply of food provided the basket is not allowed to dry out.

Plant in late spring or early summer

3 Plant the verbenas to one side of each of the dahliettas.

4 Finally plant the *Argyranthemums*, angling the plants to encourage them to trail over the edge of the basket. Water well and hang in a sunny position.

A Silver and White Wall Basket

The silvery *Helichrysum* foliage and cool blue lavender flowers give a delicate colour scheme which would look good against a weathered background.

MATERIALS
30 cm (12 in) wall basket
Sphagnum moss
Compost
Slow-release plant food granules

PLANTS
2 lavender (*Lavandula dentata* var. *candicans*)
Osteospermum 'Whirligig'
2 *Helichrysum petiolare*

Osteospermum

lavender

Helichrysum

GARDENER'S TIP
The lavender used in this project is fairly unusual – if you wish, you can substitute it with a low-growing variety such as 'Hidcote'. Keep the *Helichrysum* in check by pinching out its growing tips fairly regularly or it may take over the basket.

Plant in spring

1 Line the basket with moss.

2 Half fill the basket with the compost. Mix a half-teaspoon of plant food granules into the compost. Plant the lavenders in either corner.

3 Plant the *Osteospermum* in the centre of the basket.

4 Plant the *Helichrysum* on either side of the *Osteospermum* and angle the plants to encourage them to trail over the side of the basket. Water well and hang in a sunny spot.

A Pastel Combination

A white-flowered geranium is planted with silver *Senecio*, white *Bacopa* and pink *Diascia* to make a delicate planting scheme for this basket. This type of basket works well against a dark background.

MATERIALS
30 cm (12 in) hanging basket
Sphagnum moss
Compost
Slow-release plant food granules

PLANTS
3 *Bacopa* 'Snowflake'
3 pink *Diascia*
3 *Senecio cineraria* 'Silver Dust'
White-flowered ivy-leaved geranium
   (*Pelargonium*)

Diascia

Bacopa

geranium

Senecio

GARDENER'S TIP

When the summer is over you can save the geranium for next year by digging it up, cutting it back to about 15 cm (6 in) and potting it up. It can be over-wintered indoors or in a greenhouse. Keep fairly dry.

Plant in late spring or early summer

1 Line three-quarters of the basket with moss.

2 Partially fill the lined area with compost and plant one of the *Bacopa* into the side of the basket. Rest the rootball on the compost and gently feed the foliage through the side.

3 Plant one of the *Diascia* into the side of the basket in the same way.

4 To complete the underplanting, plant a *Senecio* into the side of the basket.

5 Line the rest of the basket with moss and top up with compost, mixing a teaspoon of slow-release plant food granules into the top of the compost. Firm well to ensure the plants in the side of the basket are securely in place. Plant the geranium (*Pelargonium*) in the centre.

6 Fill in around the geranium with the remaining plants. Water thoroughly and hang in a sunny position.

White Flowers for Summer Evenings

The papery white flowers of the petunias are underplanted with white lobelia and surrounded by silver *Helichrysum* and the delicate daisy flowers of the *Erigeron*. This basket looks wonderful in the pale light of a summer's evening – hang it near a table as a decoration for alfresco dining.

MATERIALS
30 cm (12 in) hanging basket
Sphagnum moss
Compost
Slow-release plant food granules

PLANTS
4 white lobelia
3 white petunia
Helichrysum microphyllum
3 *Erigeron mucronatus*

lobelia

petunia

Erigeron

Helichrysum

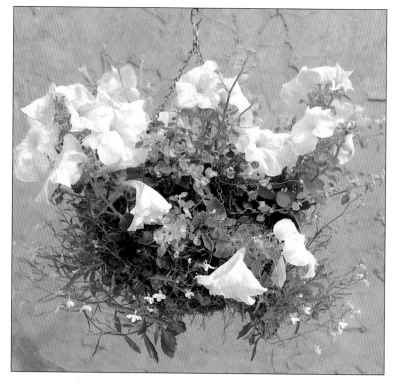

1 Half line the basket with moss and position the lobelias around the side of the basket. Rest the rootballs on the moss and gently feed the foliage through the side of the basket.

2 Finish lining the basket with moss and fill with compost. Mix a teaspoon of slow-release plant food granules into the top of the compost. Plant the petunias in the top of the basket.

3 Plant the *Helichrysum* in the middle of the basket between the petunias.

4 Plant the *Erigeron* daisies between the petunias. Water well and hang in a sunny position.

GARDENER'S TIP

Light up summer parties with night-lights in votive glasses tucked into the hanging baskets for a magical effect. Make sure that stray foliage and flowers are pushed out of the way.

Plant in late spring or early summer

An Informal Wall Basket in Silver, White and Pink

The strong pink of the dahlietta flower is echoed in the leaf colouring of the pink-flowered *Polygonum* in this country-style basket. Silver-leaved thyme and white lobelia provide a gentle contrast.

MATERIALS
36 cm (14 in) wall basket
Sphagnum moss
Compost
Slow-release plant food granules

PLANTS
5 white lobelia
3 *Polygonum* 'Pink Bubbles'
2 *Thymus* 'Silver Queen'
1 pink dahlietta (miniature dahlia)

lobelia

Thymus

Polygonum

dahlietta

GARDENER'S TIP
To prevent the thyme getting leggy, trim off all the flowerheads after flowering – this will help maintain a dense, well-shaped plant.

Plant in spring

1 Line the back and the base of the basket with moss and position three lobelias around the side of the basket near the base.

2 Plant two of the *Polygonum* into the side of the basket above the lobelia. Rest the rootballs on the moss and gently feed the foliage through the side of the basket.

3 Fill the basket with compost. Mix a half-teaspoon of slow-release plant food granules into the top of the compost. Plant the thymes into the corners of the basket, angling them so that they tumble over the sides.

4 Plant the dahlietta in the middle of the basket and the remaining *Polygonum* in front of the dahlietta. Plant the remaining lobelias. Water well and hang in a sunny position.

PINK BASKETS

Busy Lizzies in Bloom

There are not many shade-loving plants as colourful and prolific as the busy lizzie or, more correctly, *Impatiens*. A hanging basket of these plants will very happily bloom all summer long on a north-facing wall, or in any shady or partly shaded position.

MATERIALS
30 cm (12 in) hanging basket
Sphagnum moss
Compost
Slow-release plant food granules

PLANTS
6 rose-pink lobelia
3 pale pink busy lizzies (*Impatiens*)
3 white busy lizzies
3 dark pink busy lizzies

lobelia

busy lizzies

GARDENER'S TIP
In wet or windy weather, busy lizzies can look a bit battered, but once the weather improves, five minutes spent removing dead or damaged flowers will soon restore the basket to its former glory.

Plant in late spring or early summer

1 Line the lower half of the basket with moss and place three lobelias low down around the side of the basket. Rest the rootballs on the moss and arrange in the positions you prefer.

2 Carefully feed the foliage through the sides of the basket. Add on another layer of moss.

3 Plant one busy lizzie of each colour. Line the rest of the basket with moss and partly fill with compost. Mix a teaspoon of plant food granules into the top of the compost. Plant the remaining three lobelias into the side of the basket near the top edge. Add more compost.

4 Plant the remaining busy lizzies in the top of the basket. Water thoroughly and hang in partial or full shade.

A Wall Basket in Shades of Pink

Trailing rose-pink petunias provide the main structure of this wall basket and are combined with two colourful verbenas and white alyssum. On their own, the pale petunia flowers could look somewhat insipid but they are enhanced by the deeper tones of the verbenas.

MATERIALS
36 cm (14 in) wall basket
Sphagnum moss
Compost
Slow-release plant food granules

PLANTS
4 white alyssum
2 cascading rose-pink petunias
2 *Verbena* 'Pink Parfait' and
　　'Carousel', or similar

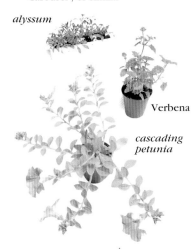

alyssum

Verbena

cascading petunia

1 Line the back of the basket and half-way up the front with moss.

GARDENER'S TIP
If, like these petunias, some of the plants are more developed than the others, pinch out the growing tips so that all the plants develop together and one variety will not smother the others.

Plant in late spring or early summer

2 Plant the alyssum into the side of the basket, resting the rootballs on the moss and feeding the foliage through the sides.

3 Fill the basket with compost and mix a half-teaspoon of slow-release plant food granules into the top of the compost. Plant the petunias in either corner of the basket.

4 Plant the verbenas, one in front of the other, in the middle of the basket. Water thoroughly and hang in a sunny position.

In the Pink

The common name for *Dianthus deltoides* is "the Pink". Its delightful deeply coloured flowers and silvery grey foliage work very well in a hanging basket combined with prostrate thymes, pink-flowered verbena and an *Osteospermum*.

MATERIALS
36 cm (14 in) hanging basket
Sphagnum moss
Compost
Slow-release plant food granules

PLANTS
6 pinks (*Dianthus deltoides*)
Osteospermum 'Pink Whirls'
Verbena 'Silver Anne'
3 thyme (*Thymus*) 'Pink Chintz' or
    similar prostrate variety

pinks

thyme

Verbena

Osteospermum

GARDENER'S TIP
Pinch out the growing tips regularly to prevent plants such as the *Osteospermum* growing too vigorously upwards and unbalancing the look of the basket. It will be bushier and more in scale with the other plants as a result.

Plant in spring

1 Line the bottom half of the basket with moss and fill with compost.

2 Plant three of the pinks into the side of the basket, resting the rootballs on the compost and feeding the leaves carefully through the wire.

3 Line the rest of the basket with moss and fill with compost. Mix a teaspoon of slow-release plant food granules into the top of the compost. Plant the *Osteospermum* in the centre of the basket.

4 Plant the verbena to one side of the *Osteospermum* on the edge of the basket.

5 Plant the thymes evenly spaced around the unplanted edge of the basket.

6 Plant the remaining three pinks between the thymes and the verbena. Water well and hang in a sunny position.

Begonias and Fuchsias

Fuchsias are wonderful hanging basket plants as they flower prolifically late into the autumn. By the end of summer, when the other plants may start to look a bit straggly, the fuchsia will be at its best with a glorious display of colour.

MATERIALS
36 cm (14 in) hanging basket
Sphagnum moss
Compost
Slow-release plant food granules

PLANTS
2 *Diascia* 'Ruby Field'
3 *Helichrysum microphyllum*
Fuchsia 'Rose Winston' or similar
   soft pink
3 deep pink begonia

begonia

Helichrysum

Diascia

Fuchsia

begonia

GARDENER'S TIP

If some of the plants in the basket begin to look straggly in comparison with the fuchsia, cut them right back and give a liquid feed – they will grow with renewed vigour and provide a wonderful autumn show.

Plant in late spring or early summer

1 Line the lower half of the basket with moss and arrange the *Diascia* and *Helichrysum* in the basket to decide where to plant each one before entangling them in the wires.

4 Fill the basket with compost. Mix a teaspoon of slow-release plant food granules into the top of the compost. Plant the fuchsia in the centre of the basket.

2 Plant the two *Diascia* into the sides of the basket by resting the rootballs on the moss and gently feeding the foliage through the wire.

3 Line the rest of the basket with moss, partly fill with compost and plant the three *Helichrysum* into the side of the basket near the rim using the same method as before.

5 Finally, plant the three begonias around the fuchsia. Water well and hang the basket in full sun or partial shade.

'Balcon' Geraniums

Traditionally planted to cascade from the balconies of houses and flats in many European countries, these lovely geraniums are now increasingly and deservedly popular. They are seen at their best when planted alone, as in the basket shown here, where the only variation is of colour.

MATERIALS
40 cm (16 in) hanging basket
Sphagnum moss
Compost
Slow-release plant food granules

PLANTS
5 'Balcon' geraniums (*Pelargonium* 'Princess of Balcon' and 'King of Balcon' were used here)

'Balcon' geraniums

GARDENER'S TIP
Take cuttings from non-flowering stems in the autumn to use in next year's basket. Geranium cuttings root easily and the young plants can be kept on a windowsill until spring.

Plant in late spring or early summer

1 Fully line the basket with moss.

2 Fill with compost. Mix a teaspoon of slow-release plant food granules into the top layer of the compost.

3 Plant one of the geraniums in the centre of the basket.

4 Plant the other four geraniums round the edge of the basket and remove any supporting canes to encourage the plants to tumble over the side. Water well and hang in a sunny spot.

Pretty in Pink and Silver

Verbena 'Pink Parfait' has a wonderful range of colours in each flower-head with deep pink petals in the centre going through a band of white to pale pink outer edges. In this basket it blends harmoniously with a soft pink geranium (*Pelargonium*) and silver *Helichrysum microphyllum*.

MATERIALS
36 cm (14 in) hanging basket
Sphagnum moss
Compost
Slow-release plant food granules

PLANTS
3 *Helichrysum microphyllum*
Pastel pink geranium (*Pelargonium*)
3 *Verbena* 'Pink Parfait'

Helichrysum

Verbena

geranium

1 Line the lower half of the basket with moss.

2 Plant the *Helichrysum* into the side of the basket by resting the rootballs on the moss and carefully feeding the foliage between the wires.

GARDENER'S TIP

Pastel-coloured baskets can appear a little one-dimensional. The addition of a deeper colour, such as *Verbena* 'Pink Parfait', will add emphasis and depth without disrupting the general colour scheme.

Plant in late spring or early summer

3 Line the rest of the basket with moss and fill with compost. Mix a teaspoon of plant food granules into the top layer of the compost. Plant the geranium in the centre of the basket.

4 Plant the verbenas around the geranium. Water thoroughly and hang in a sunny position.

A Small Basket of Geraniums

Ivy-leaved geraniums (*Pelargoniums*) are lovely plants for hanging baskets and one plant will fill a small basket like this by the middle of summer. The silver-leaved *Helichrysum* and lilac *Diascia* add the finishing touches to a pink-and-silver theme.

MATERIALS
25 cm (10 in) hanging basket
Sphagnum moss
Compost
Slow-release plant food granules

PLANTS
2 *Diascia* 'Lilac Belle'
Ivy-leaved geranium (*Pelargonium*)
    'Super Rose'
2 *Helichrysum microphyllum*

Diascia

Helichrysum

geranium

1 Line the bottom half of the hanging basket with moss.

2 Plant the *Diascia* into the side of the basket by resting the rootballs on the moss and gently feeding the foliage between the wires. Add some compost.

3 Line the rest of the basket with moss, top up with compost and mix a teaspoon of slow-release plant food granules into the top layer. Plant the geranium in the centre of the basket.

GARDENER'S TIP

If you like some height in your hanging basket, use small canes to support some of the geraniums stems; if you prefer a cascading effect, leave the geraniums unsupported.

Plant in late spring or early autumn

4 Plant the *Helichrysum* on either side of the geranium. Water well and hang in a sunny position.

Sweet Peas, Geranium and Chives

This large basket is filled with sweet peas surrounding a regal geranium (*Pelargonium*) and interplanted with chives to provide a contrasting leaf shape and help deter pests.

GARDENER'S TIP
Sweet peas will flower longer if you keep picking the flowers and be sure to remove any seed pods as they form. Similarly, the chives grow longer and stronger if their flower heads are removed before they seed.

Plant in late spring

MATERIALS
40 cm (16 in) hanging basket
Sphagnum moss
Compost
Slow-release plant food granules

PLANTS
Regal geranium (*Pelargonium*) 'Sancho Panza'
2-3 small pots or a strip of low-growing sweet peas such as 'Snoopea'
3 chive plants

sweet peas

chives

geranium

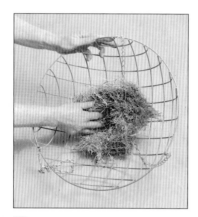

1 Line the basket with moss.

2 Fill the basket with compost and mix a teaspoon of slow-release plant food granules into the top of the compost. Plant the geranium (*Pelargonium*) in the centre of the basket.

3 Gently divide the sweet peas into clumps of about eight plants each.

4 Plant the sweet pea clumps around the edge of the basket.

5 Plant the chives between the sweet peas and the geranium.

6 Fill any gaps with a little moss. Water well and hang in a sunny position.

Good Enough to Eat

All the plants in this basket bear an edible crop; the tomato fruit, nasturtium flowers and parsley leaves. You could even impress your family or guests with a "hanging basket salad", using all three as ingredients.

MATERIALS
36 cm (14 in) hanging basket
Sphagnum moss
Compost
Slow-release plant food granules

PLANTS
6 parsley plants
5 trailing nasturtiums
3 tomatoes 'Tumbler', or similar

parsley

trailing nasturtium

tomato

GARDENER'S TIP
If you would prefer to grow your plants organically, plant this basket in an organic compost and use natural plant foods such as pelleted chicken manure and a liquid seaweed feed.

Plant in late spring or early summer

1 Line the lower half of the basket with moss.

2 Plant three parsley plants into the side of the basket by resting the rootballs on the moss and feeding the leaves through the side of the basket.

3 Put moss nearly to the lip of the basket and fill with compost. Mix a teaspoon of slow-release plant food granules into the top of the compost. Plant three nasturtium plants into the side of the basket, just below the lip.

4 Complete lining the basket with moss, being careful to tuck plenty of moss around the nasturtiums.

5 Plant the tomato plants in the top of the basket.

6 Plant the remaining three parsley plants amongst the tomatoes in the top of the basket. Water well and hang in a sunny position. Liquid feed regularly.

A Wall Basket of Contrasting Colours

The deep green and burgundy foliage of *Fuchsia* 'Thalia' will be even more startling later in summer when the bright red pendant flowers stand out against the leaves and compete with the glowing colours of the *Nemesia*. The yellow-green *Helichrysum* provides a cooling contrast.

MATERIALS
30 cm (12 in) wall basket
Sphagnum moss
Compost
Slow-release plant food granules

PLANTS
3 *Helichrysum petiolare* 'Aureum'
Fuchsia 'Thalia'
4 *Nemesia* in red, yellow and orange
    tones

Helichrysum

Nemesia

Fuchsia

GARDENER'S TIP
Dead-head the *Nemesia* regularly to ensure that they continue flowering throughout the summer.

Plant in late spring or early summer

1 Line the back of the basket and the lower half of the front with moss. Fill the lower half of the basket with compost.

3 Line the rest of the basket with moss and top up with compost. Mix a half-teaspoon of slow-release plant food granules into the top layer of compost. Plant the fuchsia in the centre of the basket.

2 Plant two of the *Helichrysum* plants into the side of the basket by resting the rootballs on the moss and carefully feeding the foliage between the wires.

4 Plant the remaining *Helichrysum* in front of the fuchsia. Plant two *Nemesia* on either side of the central plants. Water well and hang in full or partial sun.

Summer Fruits

The red of ripening strawberries is matched by vibrant red geranium (*Pelargonium*) flowers in this unusual arrangement. Alpine strawberry plants make a good contrast, with their delicate fruit and tendrils.

MATERIALS
36 cm (14 in) hanging basket
Sphagnum moss
Compost
Slow-release plant food granules

PLANTS:
3 strawberry plants 'Maxim', or
  similar
1 deep-red geranium (*Pelargonium*)
  'Miss Flora'
3 alpine strawberry plants

alpine strawberry

strawberry

geranium

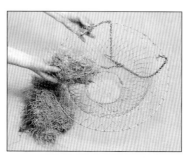

1 Line the basket with moss.

2 Fill the basket with compost. Mix a teaspoon of slow-release plant food granules into the top layer of compost. Plant the strawberry plants around the side of the basket.

3 Plant the geranium (*Pelargonium*) in the centre of the basket.

4 Plant the alpine strawberries in between the larger strawberry plants. Water well and hang in partial or full sun.

GARDENER'S TIP

After the large strawberries have fruited, cut back all the foliage on those plants to encourage the formation of next year's flowers. Keep well watered. The geranium and alpine strawberries will stop the basket looking too bare while the new foliage is growing.

Plant in spring

Fruit and Flowers

Bright red petunias become even more vibrant when interplanted with variegated *Helichrysum* and underplanted with alpine strawberries. With their delicate trailing tendrils, the strawberry plants soften the lower edge of the basket.

MATERIALS
30 cm (12 in) hanging basket
Sphagnum moss
Compost
Slow-release plant food granules

PLANTS
3 alpine strawberry plants
3 bright red petunias
3 *Helichrysum petiolare*
'Variegatum'

Helichrysum

alpine
strawberry

petunia

GARDENER'S TIP

The tendrils, or runners, sent out by the alpine strawberries are searching for somewhere to root. If you can fix a couple of pots to the wall, or the tendrils reach the ground, simply pin the plantlet into the compost or soil while it is still attached to the parent plant. As soon as it has rooted it can be cut free.

Plant in late spring or early summer

1 Line the lower half of the basket with moss.

2 Plant the alpine strawberries into the side of the basket by resting the rootballs on the moss and carefully guiding the leaves through the side of the basket.

3 Line the rest of the basket with moss and fill with compost. Mix a teaspoon of slow-release plant food granules into the top layer of compost. Plant the three petunias, evenly spaced in the top of the basket.

4 Interplant the petunias with the *Helichrysum*. Water thoroughly and hang in full or partial sun.

Vibrant Reds and Sunny Yellows

This basket is an exciting mix of glowing colours and contrasting leaf shapes. A bright red verbena and the pineapple-scented *Salvia* tumble from the basket, intertwined with red and yellow nasturtiums and a striking golden grass.

MATERIALS
36 cm (14 in) hanging basket
Sphagnum moss
Compost
Slow-release plant food granules

PLANTS
4 trailing nasturtiums
Golden grass *Hakonechloa*
  'Alboaurea', or similar
Salvia elegans
Verbena 'Lawrence Johnston'

trailing nasturtium

Verbena

Salvia

golden grass

1 Line half of the basket with moss.

3 Line the rest of the basket with moss and fill with compost. Mix a teaspoon of slow-release plant food granules into the top layer of compost. Plant the golden grass to one side of the basket.

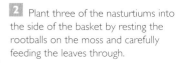

2 Plant three of the nasturtiums into the side of the basket by resting the rootballs on the moss and carefully feeding the leaves through.

4 Plant the *Salvia* a third of the way round the edge of the basket from the grass.

5 Plant the verbena at an equal distance from the *Salvia* and the grass.

GARDENER'S TIP

Nasturtiums are wonderful plants for hanging baskets, vigorous, colourful and undemanding, but they can be disfigured by blackfly. Spray at the first sign of an infestation with an insecticide which will not harm beneficial insects.

Plant in late spring or early summer

6 Plant the remaining nasturtium in the centre of the basket. Water well and hang in a sunny position.

ORANGE BASKETS

A Sunny Wall Basket

The vibrant yellows, oranges and reds of the flowers in this basket glow richly amongst the variegated leaves of the nasturtiums. As the season progresses the underplanted *Lysimachia* will bear deep yellow flowers and add another layer of colour to this basket.

MATERIALS
30 cm (12 in) wall basket
Sphagnum moss
Compost
Slow-release plant food granules

PLANTS
2 *Lysimachia congestiflora*
3 nasturtium 'Alaska'
3 mixed colour African marigolds
    (*Tagetes*)

nasturtium

Lysimachia

African marigolds

GARDENER'S TIP
If you have a large area of wall to cover, group two or three wall baskets together. This looks very effective, especially when they are planted with the same plants.

Plant in spring

1 Line the back of the basket and half-way up the front with moss.

2 Plant the *Lysimachia* into the side of the basket by resting the rootballs on the moss and carefully feeding the foliage between the wires.

3 Fill the basket with compost, mixing a half-teaspoon of slow-release plant food granules into the top layer. Plant the nasturtiums along the back of the basket.

4 Plant the African marigolds in front of the nasturtiums. Water well and hang in a sunny spot.

Mediterranean Mood

The *Lantana* is a large shrub which thrives in a Mediterranean or sub-tropical climate, but it is increasingly popular in cooler climates as a half-hardy perennial in borders and containers. This multi-coloured variety has been planted with yellow *Bidens* and orange dahliettas.

GARDENER'S TIP

To encourage a bushy plant, pinch out the growing tips of the *Lantana* regularly. Like many popular plants, the *Lantana* is poisonous, so treat it with respect and do not try eating it!

Plant in late spring or early summer

MATERIALS
36 cm (14 in) hanging basket
Sphagnum moss
Compost
Slow-release plant food granules

PLANTS
Orange/pink *Lantana*
3 orange dahliettas (miniature dahlia)
3 *Bidens aurea*

dahlietta

Bidens

Lantana

1 Line the basket with moss. Fill the basket with compost, mixing a teaspoon of slow-release plant food granules into the top layer. Plant the *Lantana* in the centre of the basket.

2 Plant the dahliettas, evenly spaced, around the *Lantana*.

3 Plant the *Bidens* between the dahliettas. Water thoroughly and hang in a sunny position.

A Miniature Cottage Garden

Part of this basket's charm is its simple planting scheme.
Pot marigolds and parsley are planted with bright blue
daisies to create a basket which would look at home on
the wall of a cottage or outside the kitchen door.

MATERIALS
36 cm (14 in) hanging basket
Sphagnum moss
Compost
Slow-release plant food granules

PLANTS
5 parsley plants
3 pot marigolds (*Calendula*) 'Gitana',
    or similar
3 *Felicia*

Felicia

parsley

pot marigolds

1 Line the lower half of the basket with moss.

2 Plant the parsley into the sides of the basket by resting the rootballs on the moss and gently feeding the foliage through the sides.

3 Line the rest of the basket with moss, carefully tucking it around the roots of the parsley.

4 Fill the basket with compost, mixing a teaspoon of slow-release plant food granules into the top layer.

5 Plant the marigolds, evenly spaced in the top of the basket.

GARDENER'S TIP

Regular dead-heading will keep the basket looking good, but allow at least one of the marigold flowers to form a seed head and you will be able to grow your own plants next year.

Plant in spring

6 Plant the *Felicia* between the marigolds. Water well and hang in full or partial sun.

Summer Carnival

The orange markings on the throats of some of the *Mimulus* flowers look wonderful with the orange-flowered geranium (*Pelargonium*) in this colourful basket. By the end of the season, trails of *Lysimachia* leaves will form a waterfall of foliage round the base.

MATERIALS
36 cm (14 in) basket
Sphagnum moss
Compost
Slow-release plant food granules

PLANTS
Orange-flowered geranium (zonal *Pelargonium*)
3 *Lysimachia nummularia* 'Aurea'
3 *Mimulus*

Mimulus

Lysimachia

geranium

GARDENER'S TIP
Dead-head the flowers regularly to encourage repeat flowering and if the *Mimulus* start to get "leggy" cut back the offending stems to a leaf joint. New shoots will soon appear.

Plant in late spring or early summer

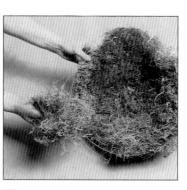

1 Line the basket with moss.

2 Fill the basket with compost, mixing a teaspoon of slow-release plant food granules into the top layer. Plant the geranium (*Pelargonium*) in the centre of the basket.

3 Plant the *Lysimachia*, evenly spaced around the edge of the basket, angling the plants to encourage them to trail over the sides.

4 Plant the *Mimulus* between the *Lysimachia*. Water thoroughly and hang in a sunny spot.

Summer Pansies with Daisies and Convolvulus

Pale orange pansies contrast beautifully with the lavender-blue *Convolvulus* and the pastel yellow *Brachycome* daisies link the whole scheme together.

MATERIALS
30 cm (12 in) hanging basket
Sphagnum moss
Compost
Slow-release plant food granules

Plants
3 orange pansies (*Viola*)
3 *Brachycome* 'Lemon Mist'
2 *Convolvulus sabatius*

Brachycome

Convolvulus

pansies

GARDENER'S TIP

Each time you water this basket be sure to remove any pansy flowers that are past their best. Once pansies start to set seed they quickly get "leggy" and stop flowering.

Plant in spring

1 Line the basket with moss.

2 Fill the basket with compost, mixing a teaspoon of slow-release plant food granules into the top layer. Plant the pansies, evenly spaced in the top of the basket.

3 Plant the *Brachycome* daisies between the pansies.

4 Plant the *Convolvulus* plants in the centre of the basket so that the tendrils can weave between the other plants. Water and hang in full or partial sun.

PEACH & APRICOT BASKETS

A Space in the Sun

Osteospermum, *Portulaca* and *Diascia* are all sun-lovers so this is definitely a basket for your sunniest spot where the plants will thrive and the colours will look their best.

MATERIALS
36 cm (14 in) hanging basket
Sphagnum moss
Compost
Slow-release plant food granules

PLANTS
6 peach *Portulaca*
Osteospermum 'Buttermilk'
3 *Diascia* 'Salmon Supreme', or
    similar

Portulaca

Diascia

Osteospermum

1 Line the lower half of the basket with moss.

2 Plant three of the *Portulaca* into the side of the basket by resting the rootball on the moss and carefully guiding the foliage between the wires.

3 Add more moss to the basket, tucking the moss carefully around the *Portulaca* plants.

4 Partly fill the basket with compost, mixing a teaspoon of slow-release plant food granules into the top layer. Plant the remaining three *Portulaca* into the side of the basket, just below the rim.

5 Complete lining the basket with moss. Plant the *Osteospermum* centrally.

GARDENER'S TIP
Keep pinching out the growing tips of the *Osteospermum* to ensure a bushy plant.

Plant in late spring or early summer

6 Plant the *Diascia* around the *Osteospermum*. Water thoroughly and hang in a sunny spot.

The Accidental Hanging Basket

Things don't always go as planned – these *Nemesia* were supposed to be orange, pink and yellow, so the blue-and-white flowers that appeared were a complete surprise. Don't worry if things don't go quite as expected – they can still look as pretty as this.

MATERIALS
36 cm (14 in) hanging basket
Sphagnum moss
Compost
Slow-release plant food granules

PLANTS
Peach-coloured begonia
5 *Nemesia*
3 *Helichrysum petiolare* 'Aureum'

Nemesia

Helichrysum

begonia

1 Line the basket with moss.

2 Fill the basket with compost, mixing a teaspoon of slow-release plant food granules into the top layer. Plant the begonia centrally in the basket.

GARDENER'S TIP
When colour schemes go awry, as happened in this instance, and you really cannot live with the results, try adding a couple of extra plants in the planned colour as this is often enough to correct the balance.

Plant in late spring or early summer

3 Plant the *Nemesia* around the edge of the basket.

4 Plant the *Helichrysum* between the begonia and the *Nemesia*. Water thoroughly and hang in full or partial sun.

A Peachy Pink Wall Basket

The vivid petunia and geranium (*Pelargonium*) flowers contrast dramatically with the greeny-yellow of the lamium. This basket is best against a dark background.

MATERIALS
30 cm (12 in) wide wall basket
Sphagnum moss
Compost
Slow-release plant food granules

PLANTS
3 *Lamium* 'Golden Nuggets'
Peach/pink geranium (zonal
    Pelargonium) 'Palais', or similar
3 petunias

Lamium

petunia

geranium

1 Line the back and lower half of the front of the basket with moss.

2 Plant the *Lamium* into the side of the basket by resting the rootball on the moss and feeding the foliage through the side of the basket. Line the rest of the basket with moss.

3 Fill the basket with compost, mixing a half-teaspoon of slow-release plant food granules into the top layer. Plant the geranium (*Pelargonium*) in the centre of the basket against the back edge.

GARDENER'S TIP

For a gentler colour scheme, the *Lamium* can be replaced with the silver-grey foliage of *Helichrysum microphyllum*.

Plant in late spring or early summer

4 Plant one petunia in each corner and the third in front of the geranium. Water well and hang on a sunny wall.

YELLOW BASKETS

A Touch of Gold

Yellow *Lantana* and the yellow-flowered variegated-leaf nasturtium provide colour from early summer onwards and later in the season the black-eyed Susan will be covered in eye-catching flowers.

MATERIALS
30 cm (12 in) hanging basket
Sphagnum moss
Compost
Slow-release plant food granules

PLANTS
3 nasturtiums 'Alaska'
Yellow *Lantana*
3 black-eyed Susans (*Thunbergia alata*)

nasturtium

black-eyed Susan

Lantana

GARDENER'S TIP
Save some of the nasturtium seeds for next year's baskets and pots – they are among the easiest of plants to grow.

Plant in late spring or early summer

1 Line the lower half of the basket with moss.

2 Plant the nasturtiums into the side of the basket by resting the rootballs on the moss and carefully guiding the leaves through the side of the basket.

3 Complete lining the basket with moss. Fill the basket with compost, mixing a teaspoon of slow-release plant food granules into the top layer.

4 Plant the *Lantana* in the centre of the basket.

5 Plant the black-eyed Susans around the *Lantana*. Water well and hang in a sunny position.

A Garland of Spring Flowers

Miniature daffodils, deep blue pansies, yellow polyanthus and variegated ivy are planted together to make a hanging basket that will flower for many weeks in early spring.

Plant in autumn if growing daffodils from bulb, and late winter or early spring for ready-grown daffodils

MATERIALS
30 cm (12 in) hanging basket
Sphagnum moss
Compost
Slow-release plant food granules

PLANTS
3 variegated ivies
5 miniature daffodil bulbs 'Tête-à-Tête', or similar
3 blue pansies (*Viola*)
2 yellow polyanthus

variegated ivy

polyanthus

pansy

miniature daffodils

1 Line the lower half of the basket with moss.

2 Plant the ivies into the side of the basket by resting the rootballs on the moss and guiding the foliage through the side of the basket.

3 Line the rest of the basket with moss and add a layer of compost to the bottom of the basket. Push the daffodil bulbs into the compost.

4 Fill the remainder of the basket with compost, mixing a teaspoon of slow-release plant food granules into the top layer. Plant the pansies in the top of the basket.

5 Plant the polyanthus between the pansies.

A Wall Basket of Tumbling Violas

Violas can be surprisingly vigorous plants and, given the space, will happily tumble over the edge of a wall basket. Combined with parsley and the daisy-like flowers of *Asteriscus,* the effect is delicate but luxuriant.

MATERIALS
30 cm (12 in) wall basket
Compost
Sphagnum moss
Slow-release plant food granules

PLANTS
5 parsley plants
5 yellow violas
Asteriscus 'Gold Coin'

parsley

viola

Asteriscus

1 Line the back and lower half of the front of the basket with moss.

2 Plant three of the parsley plants into the sides of the basket by resting the rootballs on the moss and feeding the foliage through the wires.

GARDENER'S TIP

To keep the violas flowering all summer they need regular dead-heading – the easiest way to do this is to give the plants a trim with a pair of scissors rather than trying to remove heads individually.

Plant in spring

3 Add another layer of moss and plant two of the viola plants in the wall of the basket using the same method.

4 Complete lining the basket with moss and fill with compost, mixing a half-teaspoon of slow-release plant food granules into the top layer. Plant the *Asteriscus* in the centre of the basket and surround with the remaining parsley and viola plants.

A Floral Chandelier

The chandelier shape is a result of combining the spreading *Bidens* with upright *Lantana* and marigolds. The variegated-leaf *Lantana* proved very slow to establish so a more vigorous green-leaved variety was added later. As the season progresses, the strongly marked leaves of the variegated plants will become more dominant.

MATERIALS
36 cm (14 in) hanging basket
Sphagnum moss
Compost
Slow-release plant food granules

PLANTS
3 yellow *Lantana*, 2 variegated,
    1 green-leaved
2 *Bidens ferulifolia*
5 African marigolds (*Tagetes*)

African marigolds

Lantana

Bidens

I Line the basket with moss.

2 Fill the basket with compost, mixing a teaspoon of slow-release plant food granules into the top layer. Plant the *Lantana*.

GARDENER'S TIP
To complete the chandelier, make candle holders by twisting thick garden wire around the base of yellow candles and add them to the hanging basket.

Plant in late spring or early summer

3 Plant the *Bidens* opposite one another at the edge of the basket.

4 Plant the African marigolds around the *Lantana* plants. Water thoroughly and hang in a sunny position.

Daisy Chains

The soft yellows of the marguerite flowers and foliage are emphasized by combining them with bright blue *Felicia* flowers in this summery basket.

MATERIALS
40 cm (16 in) hanging basket
Sphagnum moss
Compost
Slow-release plant food granules

PLANTS
3 variegated *Felicia*
3 yellow marguerites
   (*Argyranthemum*)
3 *Helichrysum petiolare* 'Aureum'

marguerite

Helichrysum

Felicia

1 Line the lower half of the basket with moss.

2 Plant the *Felicia* into the side of the basket by resting the rootballs on the moss and carefully guiding the foliage through the sides of the basket.

3 Line the rest of the basket with moss. Fill the basket with compost, mixing a teaspoon of slow-release plant food granules into the top layer. Plant the marguerites in the top of the basket.

4 Plant the *Helichrysum* between the marguerites, angling the plants to encourage them to grow over the edge of the basket. Water well and hang in full or partial sun.

GARDENER'S TIP

Pinch out the growing tips of the marguerites regularly to encourage bushy plants.

Plant in late spring or early summer

Small is Beautiful

Not everyone has room for a large hanging basket, especially when the plants have reached maturity, but there is sure to be space for a small basket like this one which will flower cheerfully all summer long.

MATERIALS
25 cm (10 in) hanging basket
Sphagnum moss
Compost
Slow- release plant food granules

PLANTS
4 nasturtiums
2 *Lysimachia nummularia* 'Aurea'
3 pot marigolds (*Calendula*)

nasturtium

Lysimachia

marigolds

1 Line the lower half of the basket with moss.

2 Plant three of the nasturtiums into the side of the basket by resting the rootballs on the moss and carefully guiding the leaves through the sides of the basket.

GARDENER'S TIP

Small baskets dry out very quickly so be sure to water frequently. To give a really good soak, you can immerse the basket in a bucket of water, but be careful not to damage the trailing plants.

Plant in spring

3 Line the rest of the basket with moss and fill with compost, mixing a half-teaspoon of slow-release plant food granules into the top layer. Plant the *Lysimachia* opposite one another at the edge of the basket.

4 Plant the pot marigolds in the top of the basket.

5 Plant the remaining nasturtium in the middle of the basket. Water well and hang in a sunny position.

BLUE BASKETS

Shades of Blue

Some unlikely plants, such as this powder-blue scabious, can do very well in a hanging basket, especially when combined, as it is here, with *Isotoma* and *Ageratum* in the same colour and the trailing silver foliage of *Helichrysum*.

MATERIALS
40 cm (16 in) hanging basket
Sphagnum moss
Compost
Slow-release plant food granules

PLANTS
6 blue *Ageratum*
Blue scabious
3 *Helichrysum petiolare*
3 blue *Isotoma axillaris*

Ageratum

Isotoma

Helichrysum

scabious

1 Line half of the basket with moss.

2 Plant three of the *Ageratum* into the side of the basket by resting the rootballs on the moss and carefully guiding the foliage through the side.

3 Add a further layer of moss and plant the other three *Ageratum* into the side of the basket at a higher level.

4 Fill the basket with compost, mixing a teaspoon of slow-release plant food granules into the top layer. Plant the scabious in the centre of the basket.

5 Plant the *Helichrysum* evenly spaced around the edge of the basket.

GARDENER'S TIP

At the end of the season the scabious can be removed from the basket and planted in the border to flower for many years to come.

Plant in late spring

6 Plant the *Isotoma* between the *Helichrysum*. Water well and hang in a sunny position.

A Cascade of Blue and Silver

Blue petunias and violas are surrounded by a cascading curtain of variegated ground ivy and silver-leaved *Senecio* in this softly coloured hanging basket.

MATERIALS
30 cm (12 in) hanging basket
Sphagnum moss
Compost
Slow-release plant food granules

PLANTS
3 deep blue violas
3 soft blue petunias
Variegated ground ivy (*Glechoma hederacea* 'Variegata')
3 *Senecio cineraria* 'Silver Dust'

Senecio

ground ivy

petunia

violas

1 Line the lower half of the basket with moss.

3 Line the rest of the basket with moss and fill with compost, mixing a teaspoon of slow-release plant food granules into the top layer.

2 Plant the violas in the side of the basket by resting the rootballs on the moss and carefully guiding the foliage between the wires.

4 Plant the three petunias, evenly spaced, in the top of the basket.

5 Plant the ground ivy on one side so that it trails over the edge of the basket.

GARDENER'S TIP

If the ground ivy becomes too rampant and threatens to throttle the other plants, prune it by removing some of the stems completely and reducing the length of the others.

Plant in late spring or early summer.

6 Plant the *Senecio* plants between the petunias. Water well and hang in a sunny position.

Spring Flowers

The dwarf narcissus 'Hawera' is surrounded with forget-me-nots and violas to create a delicately pretty spring display. While summer baskets need time to grow on in order to look their best, spring baskets give instant colour.

MATERIALS
30 cm (12 in) hanging basket
Sphagnum moss
Compost

PLANTS
Pot of dwarf narcissus 'Hawera', or similar
5 forget-me-not plants (*Myosotis*)
5 violas

violas

forget-me-not

narcissus

GARDENER'S TIP

Keep the narcissus bulbs for next year by re-potting them when you dismantle the basket. Leave the foliage to die down naturally and they will flower again next year.

Plant in late winter or early spring

1 Line the basket with moss.

2 Remove the narcissus from the pot and place centrally in the basket. Fill the basket around the narcissus with compost.

3 Plant the forget-me-nots around the narcissus.

4 Plant the violas around the edge of the basket. Water well and hang in sun or shade.

Sapphires for Spring

Deep blue pansies are surrounded by gentian-blue *Anagallis* and underplanted with golden *Helichrysum* in this richly coloured basket.

MATERIALS
30 cm (12 in) hanging basket
Sphagnum moss
Compost
Slow-release plant food granules

PLANTS
3 *Helichrysum petiolare* 'Aureum'
3 deep blue pansies (*Viola*)
3 blue *Anagallis*

Anagallis

Helichrysum

pansy

1 Line the lower half of the basket with moss.

2 Plant the *Helichrysum* in the sides of the basket by resting the rootballs on the moss and carefully guiding the foliage between the wires.

GARDENER'S TIP
The golden green colour of *Helichrysum petiolare* 'Aureum' is far stronger if the plants are not in full sun. Too much sun tends to fade the colouring.

Plant in spring

3 Line the rest of the basket with moss and fill with compost, mixing a teaspoon of slow-release plant food granules into the top layer. Plant the pansies, evenly spaced, in the top of the basket.

4 Plant the *Anagallis* between the pansies. Water thoroughly and hang in partial sun.

Violas and Verbena

Deep blue violas are surrounded by trailing purple verbena to make a simple but attractive basket. Trailing verbena is a particularly good hanging-basket plant with its feathery foliage and pretty flowers.

MATERIALS
30 cm (12 in) hanging basket
Sphagnum moss
Compost
Slow-release plant food granules

PLANTS
9 blue violas
3 purple trailing verbenas

trailing verbena

violas

1 Line the lower half of the basket with moss.

2 Plant five of the violas into the side of the basket by resting the rootballs on the moss and guiding the foliage through the side of the basket.

GARDENER'S TIP

If the violas grow too tall, pinch out the main stems of the plants to encourage the spreading side shoots.

Plant in spring

3 Line the rest of the basket with moss and fill with compost, mixing a teaspoon of slow-release plant food granules into the top layer. Plant the verbenas around the edge of the basket

4 Plant the remaining violas in the centre of the basket. Water well and hang in partial sun.

76

Sweet-scented Lavender

In this large basket an unusual lavender is planted amongst *Convolvulus sabatius* and the fan-shaped flowers of *Scaevola*. Underplanting ensures that the flowers cascade down the sides of the basket.

GARDENER'S TIP
If you are unable to obtain *Lavandula dentata*, then 'Hidcote' or 'Munstead' are easily available substitutes.

Plant in spring

MATERIALS
40 cm (16 in) hanging basket
Sphagnum moss
Compost
Slow-release plant food granules

PLANTS
3 *Convolvulus sabatius*
2 *Scaevola*
2 lavender (*Lavandula dentata* var. *candicans*)

lavender

Convolvulus

Scaevola

1 Line the lower half of the basket with moss.

2 Plant two of the *Convolvulus* into the side of the basket by resting the rootballs on the moss and carefully guiding the foliage between the wires.

3 Plant one of the *Scaevola* into the side of the basket in the same way.

4 Line the rest of the basket with moss, taking care to tuck the moss around the underplanted plants.

5 Fill the basket with compost, mixing a teaspoon of slow-release plant food granules into the top layer. Plant the lavenders opposite one another in the top of the basket.

6 Plant the remaining *Convolvulus* and *Scaevola* plants in the spaces between the lavenders. Water thoroughly and hang in a sunny position.

A Pastel Composition

Pure white geraniums (*Pelargoniums*) emerge from a
sea of blue *Felicia*, pinky-blue *Brachycome* daisies and
verbena in this romantic basket.

MATERIALS
36 cm (14 in) hanging basket
Sphagnum moss
Compost
Slow-release plant food granules

PLANTS
2 pink verbena
2 *Brachycome* 'Pink Mist'
Blue *Felicia*
White geranium (*Pelargonium*)

verbena

Felicia

Brachycome

geranium

1 Line the basket with moss.

2 Fill the basket with compost, mixing
a teaspoon of slow-release plant food
granules into the top layer.

3 Plant the verbenas opposite each
other at the edge of the basket, angling
the rootballs to encourage the foliage to
tumble over the sides.

4 Plant the *Brachycome* daisies around
the edge of the basket.

GARDENER'S TIP
White geranium flowers discolour as
they age; be sure to pick them off to
keep the basket looking its best.

Plant in late spring or early summer

5 Plant the *Felicia* off-centre in the middle of the basket.

6 Plant the geranium (*Pelargonium*) off-centre in the remaining space in the middle of the basket. Water thoroughly and hang in a sunny position.

Divine Magenta

The gloriously strong colour of magenta petunias is combined with blue *Convolvulus sabatius*, heliotrope, which will bear scented deep purple flowers, and a variegated scented-leaf geranium (*Pelargonium*), which will add colour and fragrance later in the summer.

MATERIALS
45 cm (18 in) basket
Sphagnum moss
Compost
Slow-release plant food granules

PLANTS
Scented-leaf geranium (*Pelargonium*)
  'Fragrans Variegatum'
3 purple heliotropes
3 *Convolvulus sabatius*
5 trailing magenta-flowered petunias

heliotropes

Convolvulus

geranium

petunia

GARDENER'S TIP

Baskets with flat bases like this one can be stood on columns rather than hung from brackets. This is a useful solution if fixing a bracket is difficult.

Plant in late spring or early summer

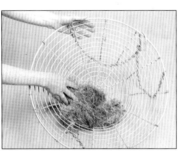
1 Line the basket with moss.

2 Fill the basket with compost, mixing a teaspoon of slow-release plant food granules into the top layer.

3 Plant the scented-leaf geranium (*Pelargonium*) in the middle of the hanging basket.

4 Plant the heliotropes, evenly spaced around the geranium.

5 Plant the *Convolvulus*, evenly spaced around the edge of the basket.

6 Plant the petunias between the *Convolvulus* and the heliotrope.

PURPLE BASKETS

Showers of Flowers

Deep, velvety purple pansies and purple sage are surrounded by pink *Nemesia* and tumbling purple-pink verbena in a pretty basket hung here in the corner of a thatched summerhouse.

MATERIALS
40 cm (16 in) hanging basket
Sphagnum moss
Compost
Slow-release plant food granules

PLANTS
3 purple verbenas
Purple sage
3 deep purple pansies (*Viola*)
6 *Nemesia* 'Confetti'

verbena

purple sage

pansy

Nemesia

1 Line the lower half of the basket with moss.

2 Plant the verbenas in the side of the basket. Line the basket with moss and fill with compost, mixing a teaspoon of plant food granules into the compost.

3 Plant the sage in the middle of the basket. Then plant the three purple pansies around the sage.

4 Add more compost around the pansies and press in firmly.

5 Plant three *Nemesia* at the back of the pansies.

6 Plant the remaining *Nemesia* between the pansies. Water thoroughly and hang in light shade or partial sun.

GARDENER'S TIP
In summer, pansies tend to flag in hot sun, especially when planted in hanging baskets. They will do best where they are in the shade during the hottest part of the day.

Plant in spring

Cascading Ivy with Dark Flowers and Foliage

Viola 'Bowles' Black' is combined with black grass – *Ophiopogon* – and the dramatically coloured *Begonia rex*. Pale pink *Nemesia* and variegated ground ivy provide an effective contrast.

MATERIALS
36 cm (14 in) hanging basket
Sphagnum moss
Compost
Slow-release plant food granules

PLANTS
Begonia rex
black grass (*Ophiopogon*)
2 variegated ground ivies (*Glechoma hederacea* 'Variegata')
2 *Nemesia* 'Confetti'
2 *Viola* 'Bowles' Black'

ground ivy

Ophiopogon

Nemesia

Viola

begonia

1 Line the basket with moss.

3 Plant the black grass in front of the begonia.

2 Fill the basket with compost, mixing a teaspoon of plant food granules into the top layer of compost. Plant the begonia at the back of the basket.

4 Plant the ground ivies at either side of the basket, angling the rootballs to encourage the foliage to tumble down the sides of the basket.

5 Plant the *Nemesia* on either side of the begonia.

GARDENER'S TIP

At the end of the season the begonia can be potted up and kept indoors as a houseplant and the black grass can be planted in an outdoor container.

Plant in late spring or early summer

6 Plant the violas on either side of the black grass. Water well and hang in light shade.

Bronze and Gold Winners

Bronze pansies and *Mimulus* and golden green *Lysimachia* take the medals in this striking arrangement, with richly coloured *Heuchera* adding to the unusual mixture of tones.

MATERIALS
40 cm (16 in) hanging basket
Sphagnum moss
Compost
Slow-release plant food granules

PLANTS
Heuchera 'Bressingham Bronze'
3 bronze-coloured pansies (*Viola*)
3 bronze-coloured *Mimulus*
3 *Lysimachia nummularia* 'Aurea'

Mimulus

pansy

Heuchera

Lysimachia

GARDENER'S TIP

At the end of the season the *Heuchera* can be planted in the border or in a container. It will do best in partial shade, as full sun tends to scorch and discolour the leaves.

Plant in spring

1 Line the basket with moss.

2 Fill the basket with compost, mixing a teaspoon of plant food granules into the top layer of compost.

3 Plant the *Heuchera* in the middle of the basket.

4 Plant the pansies, evenly spaced, around the *Heuchera*.

5 Plant the *Mimulus* between the pansies.

6 Plant the *Lysimachia* around the edge of the basket. Water well and hang in light shade.

Sugar and Spice

The candy-floss colour of the petunias is enriched by combining them with deep crimson ivy-leaved geraniums (*Pelargonium*). Slower growing silver-leaved snapdragons and a variegated geranium will add further colour later in the summer.

MATERIALS
36 cm (14 in) hanging basket
Sphagnum moss
Compost
Slow-release plant food granules

PLANTS
3 snapdragons (*Antirrhinum*)
  'Avalanche' (optional)
Ivy-leaved geranium (*Pelargonium*)
  'Blue Beard'
Ivy-leaved geranium (*Pelargonium*)
  'L'Elégante' (optional)
3 pink petunias

snapdragon

ivy-leaved geraniums

pink petunia

1 Line the lower half of the basket with moss.

2 Plant the snapdragons in the side of the basket, resting the rootballs on the moss and guiding the foliage through the side of the basket.

3 Line the remainder of the basket with moss, tucking it carefully around the underplanted snapdragons.

4 Fill the basket with compost, mixing a teaspoon of slow-release plant food granules into the top layer of compost. Plant the 'Blue Beard' geranium (*Pelargonium*) at the back of the basket.

5 Plant the 'L'Elégante' geranium at the front of the basket.

GARDENER'S TIP

It is a good idea to include a number of different plants in a hanging basket. It creates a more interesting picture and ensures that if one plant does not thrive, as happened to the snapdragons in this basket, the other plants will still make a good display

Plant in late spring or early summer

6 Plant the petunias around the geraniums. Water thoroughly and hang in a sunny position.

An Antique Wall Basket

This old wirework basket is an attractive container for a planting scheme which includes deep pink pansies, a variegated-leaf geranium (*Pelargonium*) with soft pink flowers, a blue *Convolvulus* and deep pink alyssum.

GARDENER'S TIP
Wall baskets look good amongst climbing plants, but you will need to cut and tie back the surrounding foliage if it gets too exuberant.

Plant in late spring or early summer

MATERIALS
30 cm (12 in) wall basket
Sphagnum moss
Compost
Slow-release plant food granules

PLANTS
5 rose-pink alyssum
Ivy-leaved geranium (*Pelargonium*)
  'L'Elégante'
3 deep pink pansies
Convolvulus sabatius

alyssum

1 Line the back of the basket and the lower half of the front with moss. Plant the alyssum into the side of the basket by resting the rootballs on the moss and guiding the foliage through the wires.

2 Line the remainder of the basket with moss and fill with compost, mixing a half-teaspoon of plant food granules into the top layer of compost. Plant the geranium at the front of the basket.

3 Plant the pansies around the geranium.

geranium

pansy

Convolvulus

4 Plant the *Convolvulus* at the back of the basket, trailing its foliage through the other plants. Water well and hang in partial sun.

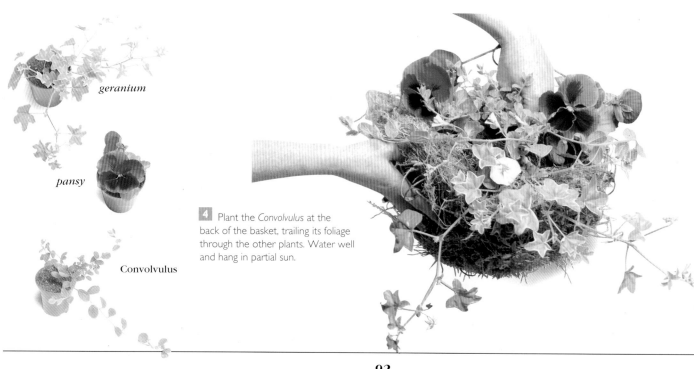

Seasonal Planting Lists

Plants for an early spring basket

Crocuses
Miniature daffodils and narcissus
Ferns
Forget-me-nots (*Myosotis*)
Ivies
Pansies
Periwinkle (*Vinca minor*)
Polyanthus
Primroses
Violas

Plants for the summer

Ageratum
Alyssum
Begonia semperflorens
Brachycome
Calendula (dwarf)
Campanula isophylla
Convolvulus sabatius
Dianthus
Diascia
Erigeron
Felicia
Fragaria
Fuchsias
Gazanias
Geranium *(Pelargonium)*
Hedera
Heliotrope
Lantana
Lavandula (dwarf)
Lobelia
Nasturtiums
Pansies
Parsley
Periwinkle (*Vinca minor*)
Petunias
Salvia
Scabiosa
Scaevola
Thymus
Verbena
Viola

Plants to last into late autumn

Begonias
Felicia
Fuchsias
Geraniums (*Pelargonium*)
Helichrysum
Salvia
Scaevola

Plants for winter hanging baskets

Convolvulus cneorum
Ivies
Pansies
Periwinkle (*Vinca minor*)
Violas

INDEX

INDEX

Marigolds see African marigold, Pot marigold
Matteuccia struthiopteris see Ferns
Mealy bugs 12
Micro-climate 6
Mimulus 54, 88
Mixed planting 91
Moisture-retaining granules 14, 15
Moss 6, 10, 11
Mottled leaves 12
Myosotis see Forget-me-not

N
Narcissus see Daffodils
Nasturtium 8, 49, 68, 94
  'Alaska' 50, 60
  trailing 42, 48
Natural predators 12, 13
Nemesia 44, 58
  'Confetti' 84, 86
Nightlights 28
North-facing walls 30

O
Ophiopogon see Black grass
Organic compost 42
Organic cultivation 42
Organic feeds 14
Organic insecticides 13, 23
Osteospermum 'Buttermilk' 56
  'Pink Whirls' 32
  'Whirligig' 25
Over-wintering 26, 36

P
Pansies 18, 55, 62, 75, 84, 88, 92, 94
  'Silver Wings' 19
Parsley 21, 22, 42, 52, 64, 94
Peat pots 8
Peat-based compost 14
Peat-free compost 14
Pelargonium see Geranium
Periwinkle (*Vinca minor*) 94
Pests 12, 23, 40
Petunias 28, 47, 59, 72, 82, 90, 94
  cascading 31
Pinching out 18, 25, 31, 32, 51, 57, 66, 76
Pinks 94
  Dianthus deltoides 32
Plant food 10, 14
Planting baskets 10, 11
Planting out 19, 71, 88
Poisonous plants 51
Polyanthus 62, 94

Polygonum 'Pink Bubbles' 29
Portulaca 56, 94
Pot marigold 68
  Calendula 'Gitana' 52
Potting compost 14
Potting-on 8
Preparation of baskets 10
Primrose 94

R
Re-using compost 12
Red spider mite 12
Regal *Pelargonium* see Geranium
Repotting 8
Rhododendron 14
Root disturbance 8
Rosemary, prostrate 22
Rot 9

S
Sage 22
  purple 84
Salvia 94
Salvia elegans 48
Scabious 70, 94
Scaevola 78, 94
Scale insects 13
Seaweed feed 14, 42
Seed compost 8
Seedlings 8
Seeds, saving 53, 60
  sowing 8
Senecio cineraria 'Silver Dust' 26, 72
Settings 25, 26, 28, 52, 59, 84
Shade-loving plants 18, 19, 20, 30, 84, 86, 88
Slow-release plant food granules 10, 11, 14, 24
Slug pellets 12
Slugs 21

Snails 12, 21
Snapdragon 'Avalanche' 90
Sphagnum moss 10, 11
Spring hanging baskets 9, 62, 74
Storing chemicals 14
Strawberries, rooting 47
Strawberry 'Maxim' 46
  alpine 46, 47
Summer hanging baskets 9
Sun, protection from 75, 84, 88
Sun-loving plants 56
Sunflower 8
Sweet pea 'Snoopea' 40
Systemic insecticides 12, 13

T
Tagetes see African marigold
Thunbergia alata see Black-eyed Susan
Thyme 94
Thyme, prostrate 32
  'Pink Chintz' 32
  'Silver Queen' 29
Thymus see Thyme
Tomato 'Tumbler' 42
Tools 15

U
Underplanting 10

V
Vegetables 21
Verbena 80, 84, 94
  'Carousel' 31
  'Lawrence Johnston' 48
  'Pink Parfait' 31, 37
  'Silver Anne' 32
  trailing 24, 76
Vine weevils 12, 13
Violas 64, 72, 74, 76, 94
  'Bowles' Black' 86

W
Wall baskets 11, 12, 18, 25, 29, 31, 59, 64, 92
Washing-up liquid 23
Water-retaining gel 9, 15
Watering 8, 9, 10, 18, 68
Weather damage 18, 30
Weight of baskets 15
Whitefly 12, 13
Winter hanging baskets 9, 18, 19

Z
Zonal *Pelargonium* see Geranium

Acknowledgements

The author would like to thank By-Pass Nurseries of Marks Tey for supplying many of the plants and taking care of the baskets until they were ready for photography. Special thanks to Priscilla, Mervyn, Margaret and Darren.

Plants supplied by:

By-Pass Nurseries
72 Ipswich Road
Colchester
CO1 2YF

Provenance Plants
1 Guessens Walk
Welwyn Garden City
Herts
AL8 6QS
(Mail order only)

Props supplied by:

Tapestry Antiques
33 Suffolk Parade
Cheltenham
Glos

SIA – The Shop
7 Montpelier Avenue
Cheltenham
Glos